Hillstrom's Hashtag Analytics

A Soup-To-Nuts Methodology For Understanding Why Social Media
Communities Grow Or Die Over Time

Kevin Hillstrom

Acknowledgements

I would like to thank Mack Collier for creating the #blogchat community. This community is a thriving social media ecosystem that is representative of an overall movement of enhanced communication between marketing professionals.

13 Digit ISBN: 978-1-4564-0662-2

Published in the United States of America by Kevin Hillstrom

Available from Amazon.com and other retailers.

Manufactured in the United States of America
First Edition

Cover Design: Kevin Hillstrom and Createspace.com
Cover Art: Kevin Hillstrom and http://istockphoto.com

Biography

Kevin Hillstrom is a database marketing veteran with more than twenty years of experience analyzing customer behavior at many of America's greatest multichannel retailers.

Kevin began his professional career in 1998 as a Statistical Analyst at the Garst Seed Company, analyzing corn and sorghum trials.

In 1990, Kevin became a Statistical Analyst at Lands' End. It was at Lands' End where Kevin learned many of the tricks and techniques required to effectively model customer behavior. Kevin worked with a very bright direct marketing team, developing experiments that explained how customers interacted with different catalog titles over time, learning all about the ways that cannibalization of marketing activities erode company profitability. Kevin ended his tenure at Lands' End in late 1995, as Manager of Analytical Services.

In 1995, Kevin became Manager of Analytical Services at Eddie Bauer. Working with an integrated database (retail, catalog, online transactions), Kevin was able to demonstrate how customer behavior changed when new stores were opened in new markets, and how customer behavior changed when new stores were opened in existing markets. As Director of Circulation, Kevin partnered with a seasoned team of Executives to deliver the most profit ever generated by the direct-to-consumer division (catalog + internet), by reducing promotions (free shipping, % off offers), reducing catalog advertising to retail and online customers, and by using advanced statistical models to target customers with appropriate direct mail offerings. It was at Eddie Bauer that Kevin developed the methodologies that would ultimately become the foundation of "Multichannel Forensics".

Following a nine month stint as a Sr. Consultant at Avenue A, Kevin became Vice President of Direct Marketing at Nordstrom. The Executive team at Nordstrom Direct was charged with turning around a business that generated more than $300,000,000 in annual sales, but was losing more than $30,000,000 in profit each year. Within just two years, Kevin and his Executive team partners were able to re-calibrate catalog contact strategies and online marketing activities, bringing the business back to break-even.

In 2003, Kevin became Vice President of Database Marketing, working in the corporate office. Kevin's team was asked to integrate outbound customer marketing strategies (direct mail, catalogs, e-mail marketing), using an integrated transactional database. In 2004, Kevin was part of a team that decided to eliminate traditional catalog marketing, a decision that was widely criticized by purveyors of existing marketing best practices. In fact, Kevin was skeptical, too. However, within twelve months of eliminating a traditional catalog marketing program, retail comp store sales continued to increase, and without the support of catalog marketing, online sales actually increased at a rapid rate. It was at Nordstrom that the final touches were put on the "Multichannel Forensics" framework that accurately suggested that retail and online channels did not need catalog mailings to support sales growth.

In March 2007, Kevin left Nordstrom to begin his own consulting practice, called "MineThatData". Kevin utilizes his Multichannel Forensics framework to help marketers understand how customers interact with products, brands, and channels. Kevin's clients include online pure-plays, thirty million dollar catalog brands, billion dollar retail multichannel brands, and international direct marketers.

Following the collapse of the economy in 2007-2008, CEOs began asking different questions, questions that focused on the long-term sales trajectory of online advertising micro-channels. Kevin expanded his Multichannel Forensics framework, resulting in what are called "Online Marketing Simulations", tools that allows CEOs, CMOs, Online Marketers, and Web Analysts to understand how online and offline customers are likely to evolve and change in the future. This information allows the online marketer to identify the "Most Valuable Path", or "MVP", the path that maps how first time buyers become loyal customers. Armed with this information, investments in keyword campaigns, affiliate marketing, and e-mail marketing change, resulting in an improved and more profitable future.

And in 2010, CEOs asked a new set of questions, questions about customer behavior. Kevin created a new segmentation methodology called "Digital Profiles", designed to combine recency, frequency, and monetary information with the channels a customer purchases from, and the merchandise divisions a customer prefers, yielding sixteen actionable segments that can be used for targeting purposes, e-mail marketing strategy, catalog circulation strategy, online targeting, and general business intelligence.

Kevin also hosts the highly popular database marketing blog, called "The MineThatData Blog", where Kevin discusses online marketing, direct marketing, database marketing, and multichannel marketing topics on a frequent basis. You can also follow Kevin on Twitter!

Contact Information:

Kevin Hillstrom
E-Mail: kevinh@minethatdata.com
Website: http://minethatdata.com
Blog: http://blog.minethatdata.com
Twitter: http://twitter.com/minethatdata

Consulting Services

Kevin provides consulting services for leading online marketers and multichannel retailers. Given his experience at leading multichannel retailers like Nordstrom, Eddie Bauer, Lands' End, and more than four-dozen consultations with direct marketers and retailers, Kevin brings more than two decades of unique executive and analytical experience to his projects.

There are many popular projects that Kevin performs for CEOs and CMOs.

- Hashtag Analytics and Digital Profiles, social media segmentation projects resulting in actionable customer personas. The segments are used for a variety of customer targeting and business intelligence initiatives across social media, mobile initiatives, retailing, and e-commerce.

- Multichannel Forensics and Online Marketing Simulation Projects, designed to determine which customers no longer need to receive catalog mailings, and outline which customers should receive a mix of e-mail marketing and catalog marketing. A typical Multichannel Forensics Project for a $75,000,000 brand results in about $250,000 to $750,000 of annual profit opportunity, well worth the average cost of a Multichannel Forensics project. A typical Multichannel Forensics or Online Marketing Simulation project takes four weeks to complete, and costs between $10,000 and $40,000, depending upon how many twelve-month buyers your business manages.

- Price Elasticity Projects, where we determine how many units of an item will sell, given different pricing strategies. You will learn which price generates the most gross margin dollars for a given item, and you will receive a spreadsheet that allows you to play with different scenarios.

- Database Marketing Audits, designed to help the CEO/CMO understand how your business stacks up against competing organizations. The typical two-day audit results in a roadmap for success, outlining database strategies and marketing strategies and staffing strategies that yield profitable outcomes.

Contact me (kevinh@minethatdata.com) for project details.

8

Introduction

Mack Collier hosts a popular social media community called "#blogchat". Every Sunday evening, a group of individuals gather to talk about a social media topic.

At some point on Sunday evening or Monday morning, we'll hear that there were 3,393 tweets, more than in any previous #blogchat event.

Intuitively, that sounds fantastic. There's no doubt that hosting a social media event with ever-increased participation is a good thing. I mean, honestly, when is the last time you were able to get five hundred or a thousand people together on your own to talk about something of interest to your community?

Outside of the #blogchat community, folks will mention metrics that illustrate the success of the event. Folks will talk about the number of followers that one social media expert earned, or will use one of a veritable plethora of social media tools to determine who the "influencers" are. Armed with information about the "influencers", marketers attempt to manipulate influencers. If the marketer can somehow encourage the influencer to say something about a product or brand or event, then those who follow the influencer will hear about the product or brand or event, giving the product/brand/event a greater chance of success.

To me, there's something about this approach that isn't quite right.

The approach suggests that if you can only get Mack Collier to say something about your product/brand/event to his loyal following, then the loyal following will evangelize the message, creating a viral effect that benefits the person trying to manipulate the influencer.

In my opinion, the approach places too much emphasis on Mack Collier, in particular. The approach suggests that one individual leads a social media ecosystem, that one individual dictates the agenda.

Unfortunately, there isn't a plethora of good data available to validate my hypothesis. We're inundated with follower counts and lists. We have a bunch of free tools that categorize us as "Everyday Users", yielding "Impact Scores" that describe one individual. That's a good thing, don't get me wrong.

But it doesn't help me understand how a social media ecosystem performs. Just because I have a low "Impact Score" doesn't mean that I am not valuable, it doesn't mean that I don't play an important role in growing a social media community.

So I embarked on a mission. I captured about four months of data from prior #blogchat events. My objectives were simple … I wanted to understand if a social media ecosystem is truly driven by a top-down approach, where a small number of influencers drove the community, or if the community drove the community?

To me, the results of my analysis were fascinating. Of course, themes of "influencers" were prevalent. In fact, anytime I chose to look at a static, small window if time (i.e. one week), I found that there were influencers who dominated the conversation.

But anytime I chose to look at the community across time, I arrived at a different conclusion. I found out that influencers come and go. I learned that the #blogchat community is vibrant, always changing, always encouraging new participants.

I learned that new participants are the fuel that drives the #blogchat ecosystem. In fact, the dynamics surrounding influencer sand new participants were so similar to the e-commerce, retail, and catalog customer consulting that I do that it became apparent that a new framework for evaluating social media communities needed to be developed.

This framework is called "Hashtag Analytics".

We can acquire data about any Twitter hashtag. The data can be formatted in a way for easy analysis. Variables are created on a weekly level, statements, re-tweets, amplifications, conversations, and links are tabulated. When one is re-tweeted or answered by another user, we tabulate that information as well. We analyze how individual participants migrate in and out of the ecosystem.

Most important, we classify users via a tool that I call "Digital Profiles". While free online Twitter analysis tools segment users into one of a half-dozen logical, instinctual segments, Digital Profiles help us understand something different about social media participants … specifically, they help us understand that participants evolve and change. From one month to another, individual participants actually migrate into different Digital Profiles, increasing their value to the community or becoming less likely to contribute in the future.

This migration, into and out of Digital Profiles, allows us to predict where a social media community might evolve to over the next few months. The ability to forecast social media community evolution is unique to Hashtag Analytics, it separates this methodology from most of the research literature that is currently available.

Within the #blogchat analysis, Hashtag Analytics demonstrate that each individual participant has value, considerable value, in fact. The analysis

10

indicated a two-way relationship. The influencer doesn't need to broadcast messages for the community to thrive. Instead, the influencer needs to offer kindness and love. By simply acknowledging a new participant who re-tweets content from an influencer, the influencer rewards the new participant, helping the new participant become more engaged. And when a new participant becomes more engaged, the entire community grows and thrives.

Hashtag Analytics can be used to demonstrate this important relationship, one that values the "little guy", the infrequent participant, demonstrating that without the infrequent participant, the entire social media ecosystem is at risk. Hashtag Analytics demonstrate that without new participants, a social media ecosystem dies, often rapidly. Heck, just ask MySpace if they've learned what happens when the fuel of new participants ends. Give Twitter and Facebook five years, and both will learn this lesson as well!

Please give Hashtag Analytics a try. I am confident that you'll find value in this way of looking at user behavior in a longitudinal manner!

Important Datasets:

Raw Data:

http://minethatdata.com/Kevin_Hillstrom_MineThatData_HashtagAnalytics_RawData.csv

Forecast Spreadsheet:

http://minethatdata.com/Kevin_Hillstrom_MineThatData_HashtagAnalytics_Forecast.xlsx

Introduction to Our Dataset

I collected data from about eighteen weeks of #blogchat events. After analyzing the behavior of the community, I reduced the dataset to five weeks of behavior. I used four weeks as the segmentation period, with one week as a prediction period. Later in this workbook, we'll review eight weeks of data, using four weeks to predict the next four weeks.

Allow me to explain the variables I am tracking in my dataset.

The first variable is called "statement". Here's what a statement looks like:

MineThatData: I am really looking forward to #blogchat tonight!

In other words, the individual is communicating a statement to the entire audience.

The second variable is called "re-tweet". This is a huge form of social currency. The person issuing the re-tweet is giving another individual credit for saying something clever, or is trying to gain attention in some way.

MineThatData: RT @mackcollier Bloggers really do a nice job of sharing interesting topics #blogchat.

The third variable is called "amplify". This happens when a user adds to the statement offered by another individual.

MineThatData: And they have unique opinions. RT @mackcollier Bloggers really do a nice job of sharing interesting topics #blogchat.

The fourth variable is called "converse". Here, one user is having a conversation with another user.

MineThatData: @mackcollier Don't you think that bloggers could do a better job of being objective? #blogchat

The fifth variable is called "link". When a person makes a statement, the person links to another article to back up the statement.

MineThatData: We covered this topic on my blog last month: http://bit.ly/dk928d #blogchat

We sum each tweet a user issues, and create a sixth variable, called "tweets".

The first set of variables describe the actions a user might partake in.

The next two variables are very important. These two variables account for feedback from other users in the community.

The seventh variable is called "RT". Each time a user is "re-tweeted", I tally one for the user in the "RT" column.

In my earlier example, @minethatdata gets a value of "1" in the "re-tweet" variable. @mackcollier gets a value of "1" in the "RT" variable, because his statement is re-tweeted.

MineThatData: RT @mackcollier Bloggers really do a nice job of sharing interesting topics #blogchat.

The eighth variable is called "ANSW". This is an important variable, because it means that the user is engaged in a conversation, and that the other person in the conversation elected to answer the user.

In our earlier example, @minethatdata gets a value of "1" in the "converse" variable, while @mackcollier gets a value of "1" in the "ANSW" variable.

MineThatData: @mackcollier Don't you think that bloggers could do a better job of being objective? #blogchat

My dataset is generated on a weekly basis. Each week, I categorize all activity in the #blogchat community, for each user participating in the #blogchat community.

Let's assume that a user, called @user, issued the following tweets.

@user: @person But don't you think that brands should be "all-in" in Social Media? #blogchat

@user: If big brands don't join the conversation, they're finished. #blogchat

@user: What do you think are the three most important things a large brand should do first? #blogchat.

@user: @person This link is very helpful. http://bit.ly/dkeo229kf #blogchat.

If this is all of the activity I can find for @user, then @user has the following profile for this week:

Profile:

    Statement = 2.
    Re-Tweet = 0.
    Amplify = 0.
    Converse = 2.
    Link = 2.
    Tweets = 4.
    RT = 0.
    ANSW = 0.

The data set has one row per @user / week combination. The dataset looks something like this:

USER	WEEK	RT	ANSW	TWEETS	STATEMENT	RETWEET	AMPLIFY	CONVERSE	LINK
User01	16	4	11	20	10	2	5	3	1
User02	14	0	0	1	0	1	0	0	1
User03	16	0	0	1	0	1	0	0	1
User03	17	1	0	1	0	1	0	0	1
User03	18	0	0	2	2	0	0	0	0
User04	18	0	6	10	2	0	0	8	0
User05	14	0	0	1	1	0	0	0	0
User05	15	3	6	23	11	9	0	3	2
User05	17	0	1	3	1	1	0	1	0
User06	18	0	0	1	0	1	0	0	1
User07	18	0	0	1	1	0	0	0	1
User08	15	0	1	1	1	0	0	0	0
User09	18	0	0	1	1	0	0	0	1
User10	16	0	0	2	0	2	0	0	1
User11	18	1	0	0	0	0	0	0	0
User12	18	0	0	1	1	0	0	0	1
User13	18	0	0	1	0	1	0	0	1
User14	15	0	0	1	0	1	0	0	1
User14	18	0	2	4	1	3	0	0	0
User15	17	0	0	1	1	0	0	0	0
User16	15	0	0	2	0	2	0	0	1
User16	16	0	0	2	0	2	0	0	0
User16	17	0	0	1	0	1	0	0	1
User16	18	0	0	1	0	1	0	0	1
User17	18	3	0	1	0	1	0	0	1
User18	16	5	0	2	0	1	1	0	2
User19	15	0	0	11	0	10	1	0	1
User19	16	0	1	4	2	0	1	1	0
User19	17	1	0	1	1	0	0	0	1
User19	18	0	0	1	1	0	0	0	0

We have a ton of flexibility when we analyze data that is formatted in this manner. We can re-shape a dataset in any of a number of ways. We can compare activity in a prior period to activity in a future timeframe.

Analyzing Prior Periods and Future Periods

I filtered the dataset, capturing user activity for the most recent five weeks that were available to me. Once I obtained the information, I began the process of re-shaping the data for analysis purposes.

I created a variable called "Engage". This variable has a 1/0 value, a "1" if the user issued at least one tweet within the #blogchat community for the week ending November 11 (week 18 in my dataset), 0 otherwise.

Next, I summarized activity for the prior four weeks, weeks ending November 4, October 28, October 21, and October 14. I created two new variables, and transformed the remaining eight variables.

New Variable = Recency ... defined as "weeks since last participation." This variable can have a value of 1, 2, 3, or 4 ... one means the user last participated one week ago, four means that the user last participated four weeks ago.

New Variable = Weeks ... a sum of the number of times the user participated in the last four weeks. This variable can have a value of 1, 2, 3, or 4 ... four means that the user participated in each of the past four weeks, one means that the user only participated in one of the past four weeks.

Statement, Re-Tweet, Amplify, Converse, Link, Tweets, RT, and ANSW are all "averaged" for the four weeks. In other words, if a user participated in each of the four weeks, and had 2 statements, 9 statements, 4 statements, and 17 statements, I calculate an average ... 8 statements per week. This process is repeated for each variable.

At this point, I have a dataset with eleven variables.

Engage: Did user engage the week of November 11 (1/0)?

Recency: Weeks since last participation (through November 4).

Weeks: Number of times user participated in past four weeks.

Tweets: Average number of tweets per week.

Statements: Average number of statements per week.

Re-Tweets: Average number of times re-tweeting other comments per week.

Amplify: Average number of times amplifying the comments of others, per week.

Converse: Average number of times conversing with others, per week.

Links: Average number of links mentioned, per week.

RT: Average number of times re-tweeted by others, per week.

ANSW: Average number of times answered by others, per week.

Finally, I transformed the last two variables, into 1/0 indicators.

RT: 1 if user was ever re-tweeted, 0 otherwise.

ANSW: 1 if user was ever answered, 0 otherwise.

This dataset provides us with a way to measure a rich set of community dynamics.

For instance, I measured "engagement", the percentage of users who participated the week ending November 11, based on "recency", the number of weeks since the user last participated. Take a look at the findings:

Recency	Users	Engage	Totals	% Totals
1	496	38.7%	192	16.7%
2	530	17.7%	94	8.2%
3	342	11.7%	40	3.5%
4	206	9.7%	20	1.7%
99	807	100.0%	807	70.0%
			1,153	

Take a look at the first row. Users who last participated the week ending November 4 (recency = 1 week) had a 38.7% chance of engaging (i.e. issuing at least one tweet with the #blogchat hashtag) during the week ending November 11. 496 users had a 38.7% engagement rate, yielding 192 users who participated during the week ending November 11.

This is a low rate. And look what happens as participation becomes more "distant" ... 17.7% of those who last participated two weeks ago engaged ... 11.7% of those who last participated three weeks ago engaged ... and 9.7% of those who last participated four weeks ago engaged.

In other words, it is really important to keep the user "engaged". If the user takes a week off, or two weeks off, the user becomes less and less likely to engage in the future.

Look at the column labeled totals. This is the number of users by segment. In total, there were 1,153 users who participated in #blogchat during the week ending November 11. Most important, 807 of the 1,153 users, 70% in total, had not participated in the past four weeks.

This is soooooooo important. The success of the #blogchat event for the week ending November 11 was largely due to the fact that 70% of those who tweeted something had not tweeted anything in the prior four weeks!

In Direct Marketing, we know that New Customer Acquisition means EVERYTHING.

In Social Media Communities, we have the first piece of evidence that New User Acquisition means A LOT!

Recency and Weeks

Let's run a query that explores engagement as a function of recency, and number of weeks the user participated in #blogchat in the past month.

Recency	Weeks	Users	Engage	Totals	% Totals
1	1	255	17.7%	45	3.9%
1	2	87	41.4%	36	3.1%
1	3	80	71.3%	57	4.9%
1	4	74	73.0%	54	4.7%
2	1	400	10.5%	42	3.6%
2	2	87	32.2%	28	2.4%
2	3	43	55.8%	24	2.1%
3	1	306	8.8%	27	2.3%
3	2	36	36.1%	13	1.1%
4	1	206	9.7%	20	1.7%
99	0	807	100.0%	807	70.0%
				1,153	

Let's begin by analyzing users with a recency of one week.

If the user participated in each of the past four weeks, the user had a 73% engagement rate.

If the user participated in three of four prior weeks, the user had a 71% engagement rate.

If the user participated in two of four prior weeks, the user had a 41% engagement rate.

If the user participated in just one of four prior weeks, the user had an 18% engagement rate.

In other words, if the user participated last week, and participated in at least three of the past four weeks, the user is probably "engaged", with a 71%+ engagement rate in the following week.

So, if I'm in charge of the #blogchat community, I want to do everything I can to keep all users active, because when the user stops making a habit of participating in #blogchat events, the user is at a risk for leaving the community altogether.

Allow me to say this again, because this is a really important finding: *If I'm in charge of the #blogchat community, I want to do everything I can to keep all users active, because when the user stops making a habit of participating in #blogchat events, the user is at a risk for leaving the community altogether.*

Notice each line in the table where weeks = 1. These are folks who only participated in one week. By recency, engagement rates are as follows:
- Recency = 1: 18% engagement rate.
- Recency = 2: 11% engagement rate.
- Recency = 3: 9% engagement rate.
- Recency = 4: 10% engagement rate.

This tells us that the infrequent or first-time participant may not have a compelling reason to engage next week. Remember, 70% of those who participated in the #blogchat for the week ending November 11 had not participated in the past four weeks, so we know that new participants represent a large share of the total community. It's becoming obvious that keeping new participants active should be a primary goal of any community.

All We Need Is Love!

It is interesting that 1,153 users participated in a recent #blogchat event, but only 154 users are considered to be "highly engaged". In some ways, this is almost like the 80/20 rule that you hear so much about!

On the other side of the "80/20" spectrum, we have 255 new users, folks who participated for the first time in at least a month. Among this audience of 255 new users, we observed an engagement rate of just 18%.

In other words, newbies are not engaged.

Maybe there are attributes that help us understand which new users have the potential to become engaged in the future. Let's explore the data, and find out if there are any attributes that lead to engagement!

First, we'll look at engagement rates by the number of tweets issued by the new user.

Tweets	Users	Engage
1	183	8.2%
2	34	29.4%
3+	38	52.6%

This is an important finding. If the first time user is compelled, for whatever reason, to issue more than one tweet, then the user is more likely to come back and engage in the future.

Check out this table, where I illustrate the likelihood of engagement next week by the activity a new user participates in:

Activity	Cases	Last Wk. Tweets	Next Wk. Engage
Statement	88	4.83	34.1%
Re-Tweet	137	2.86	14.6%
Amplify	42	7.93	31.0%
Converse	63	6.63	36.5%
Link	99	3.06	20.2%
Was Re-Tweeted	44	6.59	29.6%
Was Answered	56	7.20	41.1%
Re-Tweet, Answered = No	116	1.24	6.0%
Re-Tweet, Answered = Yes	21	11.81	61.9%

The metrics in this table are sooooooooooo important.

Look at the "re-tweet" line. The "re-tweet" is one of the kindest things you can offer in the world of Twitter. You are giving the person who issued a statement "love" by re-tweeting their comments to your audience. This is how a user gains a following, by saying something noteworthy, then having the community forward the statement to their community.

And yet, those who enter the community via a "re-tweet", those who are giving the love, are those who are least likely to come back. Does this mean that those who give a "re-tweet" and then are not thanked are offended in some way? Maybe.

Now let's look at a different situation. Look at the line that says "was answered". These are folks who said something, and then were answered by somebody in the community. These individuals had a 41% engagement rate.

So let's review a combination of activities. We'll combine re-tweets with answers ... let's see what happens:

Activity	Cases	Last Wk. Tweets	Next Wk. Engage
Re-Tweet, Answered = No	116	1.24	6.0%
Re-Tweet, Answered = Yes	21	11.81	61.9%

As the kids say, "OMG".

There is directional evidence that the simple courtesy of acknowledging the new user results in a significant increase in "engagement".

Unfortunately, this puts a significant amount of pressure on the "engaged", because their content is the content that is likely to be re-tweeted by newbies. The overall health of the community, however, requires the "engaged" to at least acknowledge newbies for their generosity. A simple act of kindness, reciprocated, yields a stronger, more vibrant, more inclusive community.

Distribution of Participants

One of the interesting aspects of any social media community is the distribution of participants.

Recall that earlier, we identified an audience of individuals who participated in three of the past four events and participated in the most recent event. These individuals are "mega participants". They had a 71%+ chance of engaging again the next week.

I'm going to do something different here.

Let's divide our population into three segments. The first segment might be called "mega participants", folks who had a recency of one week and participation in three of the past four weeks.

The second segment is "prior participants", users with at least one event in the past four weeks.

The third segment represents new/reactivated participants, users who had not participated previously in the past month.

Let's look at the distribution of activity across these three audiences for the week ending November 11.

	Mega-Participants	Other Participants	New + Reactivated
Users	112	242	904
Avg. Tweets	20.59	6.98	2.56
Avg. Statements	5.02	2.11	0.87
Avg. Re-Tweets	2.97	1.82	0.67
Avg. Amplifications	1.38	0.60	0.16
Avg. Conversations	11.42	2.52	0.87
Avg. Links	3.04	1.08	0.67
Avg. Times Re-Tweeted	6.82	1.00	0.33
Avg. Times Answered	11.10	2.43	0.93
Total Tweets	2,306	1,689	2,314
Total Statements	562	510	790
Total Re-Tweets	333	441	610
Total Amplifications	155	144	147
Total Conversations	1,279	610	783
Total Links	341	261	610
Times Re-Tweeted	764	241	302
Times Answered	1,243	589	838
% Users	8.9%	19.2%	71.9%
% Tweets	36.6%	26.8%	36.7%

The "mega participants" represent just 9% of the audience, but issue 37% of all tweets.

Conversely, newbies represent 72% of the audience, but issue just 37% of all tweets.

Look at total statements ... total statements are skewed to new users.

Look at total re-tweets ... total re-tweets are skewed to new users.

Conversations, however, are skewed to mega participants.

The biggest skew in the data happen in times re-tweeted ... notice that mega participants are the ones that are re-tweeted. In fact, the average mega participant is re-tweeted 6.82 times, and is answered 11.10 times.

Across 1,258 participants, only 112 participants are the reason for more than half of all re-tweets.

In other words, a small fraction of the audience is driving the ecosystem, when analyzing this week of information.

Looking Into the Future

Earlier in our discussion, we demonstrated that a truly "engaged" user (called a "mega participant") was somebody who participated in the most recent #blogchat, and participated in three of the last four events.

So let's run an interesting query. Let's look at users who were mega participants four weeks ago, and then measure if the mega participant maintains this level of loyalty.
- 135 "mega participants" as of four weeks ago.
- 92% participated again in the next four weeks (that's good).
- 45% maintained "mega participant" status (that's not so good).

In other words, participants are not likely to maintain "mega participant" status. So where do mega participants come from?
- 61 were prior mega participants.
- 83 were prior participants who were not mega participants.
- 33 were new/reactivated participants who had not participated in the prior four weeks.

This is important. The best participants come from all sources. Mega Participants do not stay at an elite level, the drop down, and are replaced by other participants, and by new participants.

In order to maintain the ecosystem, it is critical to constantly recruit new participants, and it is even more critical to nurture current participants so that they want to continue to participate and become "mega participants".

Digital Profiles!

Yes, that's right, it's time for Digital Profiles!

Think of Digital Profiles as a unique segmentation system designed to identify participants with similar behaviors.

It isn't terribly hard to create Digital Profiles for different users. I will briefly describe my methodology, if you are somebody who is not interested in geeky mathematics, please skip the following twelve steps!

Step 1 = Pull all users during the past four weeks.

Step 2 = Calculate Recency = Weeks since last participation in a #blogchat. Sum number of weeks the user participated over the past four weeks.

Step 3 = Calculate average tweets per week.

Step 4 = Calculate 1/0 indicators ... if user was re-tweeted and if user was answered in a week. Then, average the indicators across all weeks.

Step 5 = Calculate percentages ... percentage of tweets = statements, percentage of tweets = re-tweets, percentage of tweets = amplifications, percentage of tweets = conversations, percentage of tweets with a link.

Step 6 = Standardize each variable for each user (value - mean) / (standard deviation).

Step 7 = Run a factor analysis with recency, weeks, average tweets per week, average indicators for times retweeted and times answered, and average percentages for statements, re-tweets, amplifications, conversations, and links.

Step 8 = Choose the first three factors.

Step 9 = Use the component score coefficient matrix to score each factor.

Step 10 = Calculate the median of each factor.

Step 11 = Create three indicators ... each indicator is 1 if the factor is above the median, 0 if below the median.

Step 12 = Each combination represents a Digital Profile ... 1 1 1 = Profile #1, 1 1 0 = Profile #2, etc.

Ok, we're ready to continue!

Each #blogchat participant is assigned to one of eight Digital Profiles, based on his/her tweeting patterns during the past four weeks. Let's describe each profile next.

Profile #1 = Shaping The Conversation: These individuals are usually the most active within the #blogchat community. What sets these users apart from other active participants is their preference for starting conversations. When these folks participate, they average 9.4 tweets per week, and offer the most statements per week (3.4) of any other Digital Profile. One might think of this audience as being the "thought leaders" of a #blogchat event.

Profile #2 = May Be Interested: A subset of individuals who only participate in one of four events, but have the potential for being "conversationalists". When they do participate, their questions are answered, they make statements, and they participate in conversations.

Profile #3 = Making A Statement: These are active participants who generally don't participate in conversations. Instead, these participants make statements, they have something to say, and they are comfortable sharing their point of view.

Profile #4 = Dipping A Toe: This is an inactive Digital Profile. Basically, these users issue one statement, and then disappear, they are "dipping a toe"!

Profile #5 = Joining The Conversation: An active Digital Profile that likes to respond to conversations. These individuals are likely to issue re-tweets, to amplify tweets, and to respond to tweets.

Profile #6 = One Topic Experts: This Digital Profile is unique, in that users seem to participate in only one event during the course of the month. When they participate, they tend to respond to statements, and they are very likely to re-tweet content from others. When you have a topic where you are the expert, you want these folks to participate, because these folks will re-tweet your messages and offer oxygen to any conversation!

Profile #7 = Spreading The Word: You want these folks in your #blogchat, because their sole purpose is to spread the word! This profile represents users who are likely to re-tweet content. These users are also likely to re-tweet content with links embedded in the tweet.

Profile #8 = The Ignored: This is the saddest of all eight Digital Profiles. These participants tend to issue one tweet, and most often, it is a re-tweet of content from somebody else. Unfortunately, their re-tweet is not acknowledged, seemingly shutting down subsequent participation.

These are the eight Digital Profiles in our analysis. Let's take a look at the metrics that support my description of each Digital Profile:

Digital Profile	Shaping The Conversation	May Be Interested	Making a Statement	Dipping a Toe	Joining The Conversation	One Topic Experts	Spreading The Word	The Ignored
Number of Users	280	155	212	452	459	133	166	336
Average Weeks Since Participation	1.69	2.07	1.80	1.76	2.05	2.05	1.95	2.24
Weeks Participated in Last 4 Weeks	2.06	1.00	1.67	1.00	1.49	1.02	1.62	1.00
4 Weeks: Times Re-Tweeted	3.49	0.57	2.00	0.09	2.39	4.20	1.73	0.01
4 Weeks: Times Answered	9.46	3.64	2.34	0.11	5.31	5.79	1.54	0.04
4 Weeks: Total Tweets	19.41	7.13	7.43	1.50	12.75	7.62	8.57	1.43
4 Weeks: Total Statements	7.02	2.29	4.23	1.21	2.09	0.79	1.60	0.04
4 Weeks: Total Re-Tweets	2.21	0.49	1.31	0.12	2.92	1.11	5.08	1.28
4 Weeks: Total Amplifications	1.54	0.39	1.03	0.14	0.81	0.22	0.75	0.07
4 Weeks: Total Conversations	8.82	4.01	0.87	0.03	7.06	5.57	1.16	0.04
4 Weeks: Total Links	2.14	0.45	1.53	0.69	2.16	0.80	2.25	0.11
Avg/Wk: Times Re-Tweeted	1.69	0.57	1.20	0.09	1.60	4.12	1.07	0.01
Avg/Wk: Times Answered	4.59	3.64	1.40	0.11	3.56	5.68	0.95	0.04
Avg/Wk: Total Tweets	9.42	7.13	4.45	1.50	8.56	7.47	5.29	1.43
Avg/Wk: Total Statements	3.41	2.29	2.53	1.21	1.40	0.77	0.99	0.04
Avg/Wk: Total Re-Tweets	1.07	0.49	0.78	0.12	1.96	1.09	3.14	1.28
Avg/Wk: Total Amplifications	0.75	0.39	0.62	0.14	0.54	0.22	0.46	0.07
Avg/Wk: Total Conversations	4.28	4.01	0.52	0.03	4.74	5.46	0.72	0.04
Avg/Wk: Total Links	1.04	0.45	0.92	0.69	1.45	0.78	1.39	0.11
% Who Are Mega Participants	23%	0%	17%	0%	13%	1%	13%	0%

My descriptions make more sense, now that you see the data in this table. I like to look at the rows that outline averages per week, because these metrics give me a good idea of what a user actually does when the user participates. Remember, #blogchat is held every Sunday night, so weekly averages do a reasonable job of capturing user behavior.

Digital Profiles and Engagement

Let's see which Digital Profiles are most likely to remain active over the next four weeks.

I categorized each user, based on the Digital Profile that the user belonged to one month ago, and then calculated whether the user participated in at least one of the next four #blogchat events ... and calculated whether the user was a mega participant over the next four #blogchat events.

Here are the results:

	Users	% Engaged	% Mega Participants
Shaping The Conversation	242	62.0%	24.8%
May Be Interested	105	29.5%	7.6%
Making A Statement	148	40.5%	11.5%
Dipping A Toe	202	16.8%	1.0%
Joining The Conversation	302	38.1%	12.9%
One Topic Experts	90	25.6%	3.3%
Spreading The Word	122	41.0%	10.7%
The Ignored	223	13.0%	1.8%

It's not a surprise that the "Shaping The Conversation" Digital Profile is the most engaged, and is the Digital Profile most likely to be a "Mega Participant" in the next four weeks!

"Making A Statement", "Joining The Conversation", and "Spreading The Word" are equally likely to be engaged in the next four weeks, and are equally likely to become "Mega Participants" in the next four weeks.

Among the Digital Profiles least likely to engage in the future, take a look at "May Be Interested". These are infrequent participants who were very active during their week of participation. They have a reasonable chance of coming back and participating in the future.

Finally, take a look at "The Ignored". This is a sad consequence of the #blogchat community ... this is a group of individuals who re-tweet content, are not acknowledged, and then drop out of the community.

Digital Profiles and Future Migration

Users within a community tend to evolve and change behavior over time.

Some users become more active, while other users become less active.

In this example, we evaluate the #blogchat community over the course of two months. Only users who participated in each month are included in the table. Columns represent the Digital Profile that the user belonged to last month. Rows represent the Digital Profile that the user migrated to next month!

Migration to Next Month	Status From Last Month							
	Shaping The Conversation	May Be Interested	Making A Statement	Dipping A Toe	Joining The Conversation	One Topic Experts	Spreading The Word	The Ignored
Shaping The Conversation	65	10	12	5	21	4	5	3
May Be Interested	11	0	1	2	6	1	0	1
Making A Statement	25	4	24	9	9	4	6	3
Dipping A Toe	8	1	10	7	3	1	0	3
Joining The Conversation	23	9	3	6	51	9	16	8
One Topic Experts	9	2	1	1	4	3	3	2
Spreading The Word	8	1	8	1	11	0	13	4
The Ignored	1	4	1	3	10	1	7	5

Shaping The Conversation: These users want to "Shape The Conversation" in the future, but if they drop down in status, the will make a choice, either making statements, or joining the conversation and responding to others. These users are likely to participate again in the future.

May Be Interested: Remember, this is one of four Digital Profiles that are unlikely to participate in the future. If they do participate, they tend to "Shape The Conversation" or "Join The Conversation", both representing positive outcomes.

Making A Statement: These users migrate to "Shaping The Conversation", "Making A Statement", or "Dipping A Toe". Overall, these users like to make statements, their preference for making statements in the future does not change.

Dipping A Toe: These users have a clear preference, they are likely to migrate to "Making A Statement", "Dipping A Toe", and "Joining The Conversation". Two of those three Digital Profiles are "high-value" Digital Profiles, a good thing!

Joining The Conversation: Remember, these users like to respond to what others say, so it should not be surprising that these users are most likely to stay within the "Joining The Conversation" Digital Profile. Unfortunately, some of the users become members of "The Ignored" in the future.

One Topic Experts: The most likely migration path is to "Joining The Conversation".

Spreading The Word: Not surprisingly, the two Digital Profiles these users are likely to migrate to are "Joining The Conversation", or they stay within "Spreading The Word". These participants are helpers, they tend to not want to start conversations.

The Ignored: If "The Ignored" do come back and participate, they are likely to migrate to "Joining The Conversation", with the second most likely outcome being status maintenance in "The Ignored".

This analysis tells us that users are willing to evolve and change, but there are clear patterns that repeat. Some users like to start conversations. Some users like to respond to statements, fueling conversations. Some users like to re-tweet content and help spread the word. And we learned earlier how important it is to "give love" to those in a community. By rewarding users, future participation is increased, and future participation yields a stronger community.

How Do The Metrics Change As Users Become More Engaged?

We previously discussed the likelihood of a #blogchat user migrating from one Digital Profile to another one in the next four weeks. We'll take this concept a step further. Based on the Digital Profile that a user belongs to, we will predict whether the user will participate in at least one #blogchat in the next month, and if the user does participate, we will predict just how many times the user will tweet messages, re-tweet messages, answer questions, submit links, and receive re-tweets from others.

Here are the "re-engagement rates" for each Digital Profile, based on four recent #blogchat events.

	Users	% Engaged	% Mega Participants
Shaping The Conversation	242	62.0%	24.8%
May Be Interested	105	29.5%	7.6%
Making A Statement	148	40.5%	11.5%
Dipping A Toe	202	16.8%	1.0%
Joining The Conversation	302	38.1%	12.9%
One Topic Experts	90	25.6%	3.3%
Spreading The Word	122	41.0%	10.7%
The Ignored	223	13.0%	1.8%

If we know how likely a user is to "re-engage", and if we know the Digital Profile the user will migrate to, then we can forecast the future with reasonable accuracy.

Let's take a look at a forecast for the next sixteen weeks.

29

Digital Profile Forecast: Hashtag Analytics								Change	Re-Engagemt.
	Base	Start	Today	Month 1	Month 2	Month 3	Month 4	vs. Today	Rate
Total Participants									
Shaping The Conversation	242	242	280	322	344	353	357	27.5%	62.0%
May Be Interested	105	105	155	164	167	169	170	9.5%	29.5%
Making A Statement	148	148	212	250	265	271	273	29.0%	40.5%
Dipping A Toe	202	202	452	470	476	478	479	6.0%	16.8%
Joining The Conversation	302	302	459	516	536	544	547	19.2%	38.1%
One Topic Experts	90	90	133	141	145	146	147	10.4%	25.6%
Spreading The Word	122	122	166	186	195	198	200	20.2%	41.0%
The Ignored	223	223	336	353	358	359	360	7.1%	13.0%
Total Participants		1,434	2,193	2,403	2,485	2,518	2,532	15.5%	

For now, please ignore the "base" and "start" columns. The "today" column counts the number of #blogchat participants as of early November, when the data was originally available. Then, for each four week period of time, I use use "re-engagement rates", migration patterns (illustrated earlier), and new user counts to simulate how the community will evolve and change. Given past trends, the community is forecast to grow by 16% over the next four months, that's a good thing!

Now, let's do something interesting. Let's pretend that the number of new users will be cut in half over the next four months. I have a spot in the spreadsheet reserved for adjusting new user counts by Digital Profile. Here's what the simulation suggests for the next four months.

Digital Profile Forecast: Hashtag Analytics								Change	Re-Engagemt.
	Base	Start	Today	Month 1	Month 2	Month 3	Month 4	vs. Today	Rate
Total Participants									
Shaping The Conversation	242	242	280	245	210	193	185	-33.8%	62.0%
May Be Interested	105	105	155	97	90	87	86	-44.5%	29.5%
Making A Statement	148	148	212	186	158	146	141	-33.4%	40.5%
Dipping A Toe	202	202	452	261	247	243	241	-46.6%	16.8%
Joining The Conversation	302	302	459	349	302	285	279	-39.2%	38.1%
One Topic Experts	90	90	133	86	79	76	75	-44.0%	25.6%
Spreading The Word	122	122	166	128	112	105	102	-38.4%	41.0%
The Ignored	223	223	336	201	186	182	181	-46.1%	13.0%
Total Participants		1,434	2,193	1,552	1,384	1,318	1,291	-41.1%	

As the kids say, "OMG".

Pay close attention to this outcome. If the number of new users to the #blogchat community are reduced by 50% for the next four months, total participation will not grow by 16%, instead, it will decline by 41%.

In other words, new participants are the "oxygen" that causes the #blogchat community to thrive. Without new participants, the #blogchat community will falter.

An entire generation of analysts, marketers, and social media experts have been trained to focus efforts on real-time metrics, metrics that adequately describe "what happened".

I am introducing you to a methodology for describing "what will happen"! I believe that "what will happen" is far more interesting, because I can directly influence "what will happen".

In the case of the #blogchat community, success "will happen" if the community can recruit new participants ... and then make the new participants feel valued.

Predicting Key Performance Indicators

If we can predict how many participants we'll have, we can certainly predict how many tweets we'll have.

Here's the logic. If I know that 62% of a Digital Profile will re-engage, and I know that 10% of the 62% will end up in one specific Digital Profile, and I know that in the past, people with this behavior generate six statements, one re-tweet, and one comment, then I can replicate this behavior across all Digital Profiles, across each of four months, yielding key performance indicators for the evolution of the ecosystem!

Let's take a look at a table that outlines key performance indicators for the #blogchat community, given our five year forecast.

Total Metrics (Per 4 Weeks)	Today	Month 1	Month 2	Month 3	Month 4	Change
Weeks	2,963	3,368	3,544	3,617	3,648	23.1%
Times Re-Tweeted	3,477	4,239	4,695	4,898	4,985	43.4%
Times Answered	7,232	8,853	9,710	10,085	10,244	41.7%
Total Tweets	17,562	21,545	23,412	24,202	24,535	39.7%
Total Statements	5,107	6,168	6,700	6,932	7,030	37.7%
Total Re-Tweets	3,790	4,575	4,898	5,031	5,086	34.2%
Total Amplifications	1,319	1,605	1,747	1,808	1,833	39.0%
Total Conversations	7,478	9,358	10,241	10,613	10,769	44.0%
Total Links	2,810	3,390	3,648	3,755	3,800	35.2%
Total Mega-Participants	180	231	257	268	273	51.6%
Total Participants	2,193	2,403	2,485	2,518	2,532	15.5%
Average Metrics (Per 4 Weeks)	Today	Month 1	Month 2	Month 3	Month 4	Change
Avg. Weeks	1.351	1.402	1.426	1.436	1.441	6.6%
Avg. Times Re-Tweeted	1.586	1.764	1.890	1.945	1.969	24.2%
Avg. Times Answered	3.298	3.684	3.908	4.005	4.046	22.7%
Avg. Tweets	8.008	8.966	9.423	9.611	9.689	21.0%
Avg. Statements	2.329	2.567	2.697	2.753	2.776	19.2%
Avg. Re-Tweets	1.728	1.904	1.972	1.998	2.009	16.2%
Avg. Amplifications	0.601	0.668	0.703	0.718	0.724	20.4%
Avg. Conversations	3.410	3.895	4.122	4.214	4.253	24.7%
Avg. Links	1.281	1.411	1.468	1.491	1.501	17.1%
Avg. Mega-Participants	8.2%	9.6%	10.4%	10.7%	10.8%	31.3%

This is fascinating! Though the community grows by 16% over the course of four weeks, certain key performance indicators grow much faster. Mega

Participants, for instance, grow by 52%. This is symbolic of a community where users are gradually becoming more and more "loyal" to the weekly ritual … a subset of users cannot help themselves, they have to participate each week!

Look at total tweets, growing by 40%! Total conversations grow the fastest, at 44%. If the goal of this community is to encourage conversations, then the missing is being accomplished!

Look at averages per participant. Averages per participant are improving as well!

Ok, now we'll cut back on the number of new participants by 50%, over each of the next four months. What do you think is likely to happen?

Total Metrics (Per 4 Weeks)	Today	Month 1	Month 2	Month 3	Month 4	Change
Weeks	2,963	2,402	2,079	1,937	1,878	-36.6%
Times Re-Tweeted	3,477	3,815	3,182	2,810	2,646	-23.9%
Times Answered	7,232	7,758	6,408	5,707	5,403	-25.3%
Total Tweets	17,562	18,328	15,018	13,492	12,852	-26.8%
Total Statements	5,107	5,188	4,308	3,876	3,688	-27.8%
Total Re-Tweets	3,790	3,684	3,010	2,747	2,640	-30.3%
Total Amplifications	1,319	1,353	1,124	1,010	961	-27.1%
Total Conversations	7,478	8,242	6,688	5,961	5,659	-24.3%
Total Links	2,810	2,752	2,274	2,066	1,979	-29.6%
Total Mega-Participants	180	214	174	153	145	-19.7%
Total Participants	2,193	1,552	1,384	1,318	1,291	-41.1%

Average Metrics (Per 4 Weeks)	Today	Month 1	Month 2	Month 3	Month 4	Change
Avg. Weeks	1.351	1.548	1.502	1.470	1.455	7.7%
Avg. Times Re-Tweeted	1.586	2.458	2.300	2.132	2.050	29.3%
Avg. Times Answered	3.298	4.997	4.632	4.330	4.186	26.9%
Avg. Tweets	8.008	11.807	10.854	10.237	9.957	24.3%
Avg. Statements	2.329	3.342	3.113	2.941	2.857	22.7%
Avg. Re-Tweets	1.728	2.373	2.176	2.084	2.045	18.3%
Avg. Amplifications	0.601	0.871	0.813	0.766	0.745	23.8%
Avg. Conversations	3.410	5.310	4.834	4.523	4.384	28.6%
Avg. Links	1.281	1.773	1.644	1.567	1.533	19.6%
Avg. Mega-Participants	8.2%	13.8%	12.6%	11.6%	11.2%	36.4%

This time, we see divergent trends.

Total tweets and various types of tweets decline, rapidly, with re-tweets declining the most.

Averages, however, increase, and they increase at a rate faster than when new participants are added at normal rates. This happens because "newbies" aren't being added to the community, leaving only the most loyal participants, those who contribute the most.

If the #blogchat community fails to recruit new participants at high rates, the overall community is destined to struggle. We know this, because our simulations/forecasts paint a negative trend when new participant counts are cut in half.

Residual Value

We demonstrated how changes in new participants influence the future health of a social media ecosystem.

We can also demonstrate how an improvement in any one time period impacts future time periods. This is an important topic! We use classic, point-in-time metrics (followers, tweets) to measure how effective our efforts are. But point-in-time metrics fail to illustrate how the community will evolve in change in the future. If I have additional tweets this week, does that mean that I'll have additional tweets in next week's #blogchat event, or did I simply have a good week?

We can understand these dynamics using our analysis framework.

Let's conduct an experiment. We will increase the number of new users for just one week, by 100%.

Here are the metrics surrounding our base case.

Digital Profile Forecast: Hashtag Analytics

Total Participants	Base	Start	Today	Month 1	Month 2	Month 3	Month 4	Change vs. Today
Shaping The Conversation	242	242	280	322	344	353	357	27.5%
May Be Interested	105	105	155	164	167	169	170	9.5%
Making A Statement	148	148	212	250	265	271	273	29.0%
Dipping A Toe	202	202	452	470	476	478	479	6.0%
Joining The Conversation	302	302	459	516	536	544	547	19.2%
One Topic Experts	90	90	133	141	145	146	147	10.4%
Spreading The Word	122	122	166	186	195	198	200	20.2%
The Ignored	223	223	336	353	358	359	360	7.1%
Total Participants		1,434	2,193	2,403	2,485	2,518	2,532	15.5%

Newbies		Today	Month 1	Month 2	Month 3	Month 4
Shaping The Conversation	155	155	155	155	155	155
May Be Interested	133	133	133	133	133	133
Making A Statement	128	128	128	128	128	128
Dipping A Toe	419	419	419	419	419	419
Joining The Conversation	334	334	334	334	334	334
One Topic Experts	111	111	111	111	111	111
Spreading The Word	117	117	117	117	117	117
The Ignored	304	304	304	304	304	304

Total Metrics (Per 4 Weeks)	Today	Month 1	Month 2	Month 3	Month 4	Change
Weeks	2,963	3,368	3,544	3,617	3,648	23.1%
Times Re-Tweeted	3,477	4,239	4,695	4,898	4,985	43.4%
Times Answered	7,232	8,853	9,710	10,085	10,244	41.7%
Total Tweets	17,562	21,545	23,412	24,202	24,535	39.7%
Total Statements	5,107	6,168	6,700	6,932	7,030	37.7%
Total Re-Tweets	3,790	4,575	4,898	5,031	5,086	34.2%
Total Amplifications	1,319	1,605	1,747	1,808	1,833	39.0%
Total Conversations	7,478	9,358	10,241	10,613	10,769	44.0%
Total Links	2,810	3,390	3,648	3,755	3,800	35.2%
Total Mega-Participants	180	231	257	268	273	51.6%
Total Participants	2,193	2,403	2,485	2,518	2,532	15.5%

Average Metrics (Per 4 Weeks)	Today	Month 1	Month 2	Month 3	Month 4	Change
Avg. Weeks	1.351	1.402	1.426	1.436	1.441	6.6%
Avg. Times Re-Tweeted	1.586	1.764	1.890	1.945	1.969	24.2%
Avg. Times Answered	3.298	3.684	3.908	4.005	4.046	22.7%
Avg. Tweets	8.008	8.966	9.423	9.611	9.689	21.0%
Avg. Statements	2.329	2.567	2.697	2.753	2.776	19.2%
Avg. Re-Tweets	1.728	1.904	1.972	1.998	2.009	16.2%
Avg. Amplifications	0.601	0.668	0.703	0.718	0.724	20.4%
Avg. Conversations	3.410	3.895	4.122	4.214	4.253	24.7%
Avg. Links	1.281	1.411	1.468	1.491	1.501	17.1%
Avg. Mega-Participants	8.2%	9.6%	10.4%	10.7%	10.8%	31.3%

This is our base case. Now, we'll go into the spreadsheet, and we will double the number of new users in month one. What happens to the ecosystem during the next three months? Here we go!

Digital Profile Forecast: Hashtag Analytics

Total Participants	Base	Start	Today	Month 1	Month 2	Month 3	Month 4	Change vs. Today
Shaping The Conversation	242	242	280	477	456	406	380	35.7%
May Be Interested	105	105	155	297	189	178	174	11.9%
Making A Statement	148	148	212	378	350	307	289	36.1%
Dipping A Toe	202	202	452	889	514	491	484	7.2%
Joining The Conversation	302	302	459	850	671	592	566	23.3%
One Topic Experts	90	90	133	252	166	155	151	13.2%
Spreading The Word	122	122	166	303	244	218	208	25.1%
The Ignored	223	223	336	657	396	370	364	8.3%
Total Participants		1,434	2,193	4,104	2,985	2,717	2,615	19.2%

Newbies		Today	Month 1	Month 2	Month 3	Month 4
Shaping The Conversation	155	155	310	155	155	155
May Be Interested	133	133	266	133	133	133
Making A Statement	128	128	256	128	128	128
Dipping A Toe	419	419	838	419	419	419
Joining The Conversation	334	334	668	334	334	334
One Topic Experts	111	111	222	111	111	111
Spreading The Word	117	117	234	117	117	117
The Ignored	304	304	608	304	304	304

Total Metrics (Per 4 Weeks)	Today	Month 1	Month 2	Month 3	Month 4	Change
Weeks	2,963	5,300	4,542	4,047	3,828	29.2%
Times Re-Tweeted	3,477	5,087	6,873	6,048	5,488	57.8%
Times Answered	7,232	11,044	14,121	12,238	11,171	54.5%
Total Tweets	17,562	27,978	33,766	28,836	26,481	50.8%
Total Statements	5,107	8,128	9,524	8,260	7,602	48.8%
Total Re-Tweets	3,790	6,357	6,892	5,823	5,411	42.8%
Total Amplifications	1,319	2,109	2,489	2,158	1,981	50.2%
Total Conversations	7,478	11,589	15,115	12,811	11,686	56.3%
Total Links	2,810	4,667	5,119	4,388	4,063	44.6%
Total Mega-Participants	180	265	389	332	300	66.6%
Total Participants	2,193	4,104	2,985	2,717	2,615	19.2%

Average Metrics (Per 4 Weeks)	Today	Month 1	Month 2	Month 3	Month 4	Change
Avg. Weeks	1.351	1.292	1.521	1.490	1.464	8.4%
Avg. Times Re-Tweeted	1.586	1.240	2.302	2.226	2.099	32.4%
Avg. Times Answered	3.298	2.691	4.730	4.504	4.272	29.6%
Avg. Tweets	8.008	6.817	11.311	10.613	10.128	26.5%
Avg. Statements	2.329	1.981	3.190	3.040	2.907	24.8%
Avg. Re-Tweets	1.728	1.549	2.309	2.143	2.070	19.8%
Avg. Amplifications	0.601	0.514	0.834	0.794	0.758	26.0%
Avg. Conversations	3.410	2.824	5.063	4.715	4.469	31.1%
Avg. Links	1.281	1.137	1.715	1.615	1.554	21.3%
Avg. Mega-Participants	8.2%	6.5%	13.0%	12.2%	11.5%	39.7%

Let's just look at the "total tweets" line.

	Base Case	More Newbies	Increase	Lift
Today	17,562	17,562	0	0.0%
Month = 1	21,545	27,978	6,433	29.9%
Month = 2	23,412	33,766	10,354	44.2%
Month = 3	24,202	28,836	4,634	19.1%
Month = 4	24,535	26,481	1,946	7.9%

In the first month, when we have a 100% increase of new participants, we have a 30% increase in total tweets.

More important, we get a 44% increase in tweets in month two! This is fascinating, in large part because our new users move into healthier and more active Digital Profiles. The biggest increases in activity happen in the month after new participants join the community. Residual effects continue in month three, then begin to revert back to the baseline in the fourth month.

That's what happens to total tweets. Let's look at what happens to the number of times that users are re-tweeted.

	Base Case	More Newbies	Increase	Lift
Today	3,477	3,477	0	0.0%
Month = 1	4,237	5,087	850	20.1%
Month = 2	4,695	6,873	2,178	46.4%
Month = 3	4,898	6,048	1,150	23.5%
Month = 4	4,985	5,488	503	10.1%

Usually, the most popular and most brilliant participants are those who are re-tweeted. Obviously, it takes time for these users to achieve a position of "authority". As you can see in the table, the increase in new users in month one is associated with a growth rate in "times re-tweeted" that happens a bit later than the growth rate in "total tweets".

Participant Digital Profile Membership Matters

Let's try a couple of experiments.

Obviously, we have our base case, one that illustrates where we think the #blogchat community is heading.

Now, instead of growing all new participants by the same rate, let's try something different. We'll grow the number of new users within one Digital Profile by two hundred users, each month, for four months.

Let's start by increasing the number of new "Dipping A Toe" users by two hundred per month, every month.

Digital Profile Forecast: Hashtag Analytics

	Base	Start	Today	Month 1	Month 2	Month 3	Month 4	Change vs. Today
Total Participants								
Shaping The Conversation	242	242	280	322	349	361	366	30.8%
May Be Interested	105	105	155	164	169	171	172	11.2%
Making A Statement	148	148	212	250	273	282	286	34.9%
Dipping A Toe	202	202	452	670	683	686	687	52.1%
Joining The Conversation	302	302	459	516	542	552	556	21.2%
One Topic Experts	90	90	133	141	146	148	148	11.6%
Spreading The Word	122	122	166	186	196	200	202	21.7%
The Ignored	223	223	336	353	360	363	364	8.2%
Total Participants		1,434	2,193	2,603	2,718	2,764	2,782	26.9%

	Base		Today	Month 1	Month 2	Month 3	Month 4	
Newbies								
Shaping The Conversation	155		155	155	155	155	155	
May Be Interested	133		133	133	133	133	133	
Making A Statement	128		128	128	128	128	128	
Dipping A Toe	419		419	619	619	619	619	
Joining The Conversation	334		334	334	334	334	334	
One Topic Experts	111		111	111	111	111	111	
Spreading The Word	117		117	117	117	117	117	
The Ignored	304		304	304	304	304	304	

	Today	Month 1	Month 2	Month 3	Month 4	Change
Total Metrics (Per 4 Weeks)						
Weeks	2,963	3,568	3,790	3,888	3,929	32.6%
Times Re-Tweeted	3,477	4,258	4,730	4,990	5,105	46.8%
Times Answered	7,232	8,876	9,801	10,282	10,493	45.1%
Total Tweets	17,562	21,837	23,880	24,903	25,344	44.3%
Total Statements	5,107	6,405	7,016	7,319	7,450	45.9%
Total Re-Tweets	3,790	4,596	4,957	5,129	5,203	37.3%
Total Amplifications	1,319	1,633	1,780	1,860	1,894	43.6%
Total Conversations	7,478	9,364	10,302	10,778	10,984	46.9%
Total Links	2,810	3,529	3,825	3,966	4,026	43.3%
Total Mega-Participants	180	231	259	274	280	55.5%
Total Participants	2,193	2,603	2,718	2,764	2,782	26.9%

	Today	Month 1	Month 2	Month 3	Month 4	Change
Average Metrics (Per 4 Weeks)						
Avg. Weeks	1.351	1.371	1.394	1.407	1.412	4.5%
Avg. Times Re-Tweeted	1.586	1.636	1.740	1.806	1.835	15.7%
Avg. Times Answered	3.298	3.410	3.606	3.720	3.771	14.3%
Avg. Tweets	8.008	8.390	8.785	9.011	9.109	13.7%
Avg. Statements	2.329	2.461	2.581	2.648	2.677	15.0%
Avg. Re-Tweets	1.728	1.766	1.824	1.856	1.870	8.2%
Avg. Amplifications	0.601	0.627	0.655	0.673	0.681	13.2%
Avg. Conversations	3.410	3.598	3.790	3.900	3.947	15.8%
Avg. Links	1.281	1.356	1.407	1.435	1.447	12.9%
Avg. Mega-Participants	8.2%	8.9%	9.5%	9.9%	10.1%	22.5%

Let's keep our analysis simple, we'll review the number of total tweets.

	Base Case	More Newbies	Increase	Lift
Today	17,562	17,562	0	0.0%
Month = 1	21,545	21,837	292	1.4%
Month = 2	23,412	23,880	468	2.0%
Month = 3	24,202	24,903	701	2.9%
Month = 4	24,535	25,344	809	3.3%

Growth in the community, measured via total tweets, is steady.

Now, instead, we'll add 200 new users, per month, to "May Be Interested".
The following table compares total tweets against our base case. The next table
shows what happens to the total ecosystem.

	Base Case	More Newbies	Increase	Lift
Today	17,562	17,562	0	0.0%
Month = 1	21,545	22,916	1,371	6.4%
Month = 2	23,412	25,656	2,244	9.6%
Month = 3	24,202	27,075	2,873	11.9%
Month = 4	24,535	27,660	3,125	12.7%

Digital Profile Forecast: Hashtag Analytics

Total Participants	Base	Start	Today	Month 1	Month 2	Month 3	Month 4	Change vs. Today
Shaping The Conversation	242	242	280	322	363	379	386	38.0%
May Be Interested	105	105	155	364	367	370	372	139.7%
Making A Statement	148	148	212	250	272	283	287	35.4%
Dipping A Toe	202	202	452	470	478	481	483	6.9%
Joining The Conversation	302	302	459	516	553	567	572	24.7%
One Topic Experts	90	90	133	141	149	151	152	14.5%
Spreading The Word	122	122	166	186	197	202	205	23.2%
The Ignored	223	223	336	353	365	368	369	9.8%
Total Participants		1,434	2,193	2,603	2,744	2,802	2,826	28.9%

Newbies		Today	Month 1	Month 2	Month 3	Month 4	
Shaping The Conversation	155	155	155	155	155	155	
May Be Interested	133	133	333	333	333	333	
Making A Statement	128	128	128	128	128	128	
Dipping A Toe	419	419	419	419	419	419	
Joining The Conversation	334	334	334	334	334	334	
One Topic Experts	111	111	111	111	111	111	
Spreading The Word	117	117	117	117	117	117	
The Ignored	304	304	304	304	304	304	

Total Metrics (Per 4 Weeks)	Today	Month 1	Month 2	Month 3	Month 4	Change
Weeks	2,963	3,568	3,858	3,986	4,040	36.3%
Times Re-Tweeted	3,477	4,355	4,896	5,272	5,425	56.0%
Times Answered	7,232	9,555	10,829	11,520	11,802	63.2%
Total Tweets	17,562	22,916	25,636	27,075	27,660	57.5%
Total Statements	5,107	6,626	7,431	7,852	8,025	57.1%
Total Re-Tweets	3,790	4,662	5,134	5,366	5,462	44.1%
Total Amplifications	1,319	1,682	1,887	1,995	2,039	54.6%
Total Conversations	7,478	10,119	11,381	12,070	12,346	65.1%
Total Links	2,810	3,478	3,825	4,016	4,094	45.7%
Total Mega-Participants	180	231	273	292	300	66.6%
Total Participants	2,193	2,603	2,744	2,802	2,826	28.9%

Average Metrics (Per 4 Weeks)	Today	Month 1	Month 2	Month 3	Month 4	Change
Avg. Weeks	1.351	1.371	1.406	1.423	1.429	5.8%
Avg. Times Re-Tweeted	1.586	1.673	1.785	1.882	1.920	21.1%
Avg. Times Answered	3.298	3.671	3.947	4.112	4.176	26.6%
Avg. Tweets	8.008	8.804	9.344	9.664	9.787	22.2%
Avg. Statements	2.329	2.546	2.708	2.802	2.840	21.9%
Avg. Re-Tweets	1.728	1.791	1.871	1.915	1.933	11.8%
Avg. Amplifications	0.601	0.646	0.688	0.712	0.721	19.9%
Avg. Conversations	3.410	3.888	4.148	4.308	4.368	28.1%
Avg. Links	1.281	1.336	1.394	1.433	1.449	13.0%
Avg. Mega-Participants	8.2%	8.9%	9.9%	10.4%	10.6%	29.3%

Clearly, it is better for the community to encourage new user participation among folks who "May Be Interested" than among new users who are "Dipping A Toe"!

Finally, let's review the tables for "The Ignored". Remember, this audience re-tweets content, but is not acknowledged for their kindness.

Digital Profile Forecast: Hashtag Analytics

Total Participants	Base	Start	Today	Month 1	Month 2	Month 3	Month 4	Change vs. Today
Shaping The Conversation	242	242	280	322	346	358	362	29.4%
May Be Interested	105	105	155	164	168	170	171	10.4%
Making A Statement	148	148	212	250	267	275	278	31.2%
Dipping A Toe	202	202	452	470	479	481	482	6.7%
Joining The Conversation	302	302	459	516	543	554	558	21.5%
One Topic Experts	90	90	133	141	147	148	149	12.1%
Spreading The Word	122	122	166	186	198	203	205	23.2%
The Ignored	223	223	336	553	562	564	565	68.2%
Total Participants		1,434	2,193	2,603	2,711	2,753	2,771	26.3%

Newbies			Today	Month 1	Month 2	Month 3	Month 4	
Shaping The Conversation	155		155	155	155	155	155	
May Be Interested	133		133	133	133	133	133	
Making A Statement	128		128	128	128	128	128	
Dipping A Toe	419		419	419	419	419	419	
Joining The Conversation	334		334	334	334	334	334	
One Topic Experts	111		111	111	111	111	111	
Spreading The Word	117		117	117	117	117	117	
The Ignored	304		304	504	504	504	504	

Total Metrics (Per 4 Weeks)	Today	Month 1	Month 2	Month 3	Month 4	Change
Weeks	2,963	3,568	3,784	3,876	3,914	32.1%
Times Re-Tweeted	3,477	4,241	4,817	5,061	5,168	48.6%
Times Answered	7,232	8,862	9,860	10,315	10,512	45.4%
Total Tweets	17,562	21,834	24,311	25,293	25,707	46.4%
Total Statements	5,107	6,178	6,880	7,162	7,283	42.6%
Total Re-Tweets	3,790	4,832	5,356	5,527	5,597	47.7%
Total Amplifications	1,319	1,619	1,824	1,898	1,929	46.3%
Total Conversations	7,478	9,366	10,430	10,893	11,088	48.3%
Total Links	2,810	3,411	3,808	3,942	3,999	42.3%
Total Mega-Participants	180	231	261	274	280	55.6%
Total Participants	2,193	2,603	2,711	2,753	2,771	26.3%

Average Metrics (Per 4 Weeks)	Today	Month 1	Month 2	Month 3	Month 4	Change
Avg. Weeks	1.351	1.371	1.396	1.408	1.413	4.6%
Avg. Times Re-Tweeted	1.586	1.629	1.777	1.838	1.865	17.6%
Avg. Times Answered	3.298	3.405	3.638	3.747	3.794	15.1%
Avg. Tweets	8.008	8.388	8.969	9.188	9.279	15.9%
Avg. Statements	2.329	2.373	2.538	2.601	2.629	12.9%
Avg. Re-Tweets	1.728	1.856	1.976	2.008	2.020	16.9%
Avg. Amplifications	0.601	0.622	0.673	0.689	0.696	15.8%
Avg. Conversations	3.410	3.599	3.848	3.957	4.002	17.4%
Avg. Links	1.281	1.310	1.405	1.432	1.443	12.6%
Avg. Mega-Participants	8.2%	8.9%	9.6%	10.0%	10.1%	23.2%

And here's the table comparing total tweets to the base case.

	Base Case	More Newbies	Increase	Lift
Today	17,562	17,562	0	0.0%
Month = 1	21,545	21,834	289	1.3%
Month = 2	23,412	24,311	899	3.8%
Month = 3	24,202	25,293	1,091	4.5%
Month = 4	24,535	25,707	1,172	4.8%

Once again, growth is modest.

I did a separate analysis. If "The Ignored" are not ignored, if these users are instead given recognition for their efforts, then the user migrates to a new Digital Profile. The user becomes a member of "Spreading The Word".

So, we'll run another experiment. Instead of two hundred newbies in "The Ignored" per month, for four months, why not assume that we give these folks love, causing these individuals to be in the "Spreading The Word" Digital Profile?

The results are very positive!

	Base Case	More Newbies	Increase	Lift
Today	17,562	17,562	0	0.0%
Month = 1	21,545	22,297	752	3.5%
Month = 2	23,412	25,238	1,826	7.8%
Month = 3	24,202	26,691	2,489	10.3%
Month = 4	24,535	27,305	2,770	11.3%

By giving users "love", users become more engaged, and the entire ecosystem, as a result, thrives!

Here are all of the key performance indicators.

Digital Profile Forecast: Hashtag Analytics

Total Participants	Base	Start	Today	Month 1	Month 2	Month 3	Month 4	Change vs. Today
Shaping The Conversation	242	242	280	322	352	367	374	33.7%
May Be Interested	105	105	155	164	167	170	171	10.5%
Making A Statement	148	148	212	250	274	285	290	36.8%
Dipping A Toe	202	202	452	470	476	479	481	6.4%
Joining The Conversation	302	302	459	516	562	579	586	27.6%
One Topic Experts	90	90	133	141	150	152	154	15.5%
Spreading The Word	122	122	166	386	416	424	427	157.0%
The Ignored	223	223	336	353	369	373	375	11.5%
Total Participants		1,434	2,193	2,603	2,766	2,831	2,857	30.3%

Newbies	Base		Today	Month 1	Month 2	Month 3	Month 4	
Shaping The Conversation	155		155	155	155	155	155	
May Be Interested	133		133	133	133	133	133	
Making A Statement	128		128	128	128	128	128	
Dipping A Toe	419		419	419	419	419	419	
Joining The Conversation	334		334	334	334	334	334	
One Topic Experts	111		111	111	111	111	111	
Spreading The Word	117		117	317	317	317	317	
The Ignored	304		304	304	304	304	304	

Total Metrics (Per 4 Weeks)	Today	Month 1	Month 2	Month 3	Month 4	Change
Weeks	2,963	3,630	3,971	4,109	4,166	40.6%
Times Re-Tweeted	3,477	4,445	5,072	5,413	5,567	60.1%
Times Answered	7,232	8,985	10,097	10,738	11,025	52.4%
Total Tweets	17,562	22,297	25,238	26,691	27,305	55.5%
Total Statements	5,107	6,265	6,996	7,392	7,568	48.2%
Total Re-Tweets	3,790	5,141	6,008	6,289	6,396	68.8%
Total Amplifications	1,319	1,641	1,844	1,952	1,998	51.5%
Total Conversations	7,478	9,414	10,576	11,256	11,546	54.4%
Total Links	2,810	3,584	4,089	4,296	4,379	55.9%
Total Mega-Participants	180	242	289	309	318	76.4%
Total Participants	2,193	2,603	2,766	2,831	2,857	30.3%

Average Metrics (Per 4 Weeks)	Today	Month 1	Month 2	Month 3	Month 4	Change
Avg. Weeks	1.351	1.395	1.435	1.451	1.458	7.9%
Avg. Times Re-Tweeted	1.586	1.708	1.833	1.912	1.949	22.9%
Avg. Times Answered	3.298	3.452	3.650	3.793	3.859	17.0%
Avg. Tweets	8.008	8.566	9.123	9.429	9.558	19.3%
Avg. Statements	2.329	2.407	2.529	2.611	2.649	13.8%
Avg. Re-Tweets	1.728	1.975	2.172	2.222	2.239	29.5%
Avg. Amplifications	0.601	0.630	0.667	0.689	0.699	16.3%
Avg. Conversations	3.410	3.617	3.823	3.976	4.041	18.5%
Avg. Links	1.281	1.377	1.478	1.517	1.533	19.6%
Avg. Mega-Participants	8.2%	9.3%	10.4%	10.9%	11.1%	35.4%

The amazing thing about this community is that there are "feedback loops". We've probably always known this, in general, but within this community, strength comes from individuals giving positive feedback to each other. Positive feedback yields stronger, more active participants. Active participants are stronger, yielding stronger #blogchat events. Stronger #blogchat events attract more participants. This feedback loop continues.

It is up to individuals to provide support for each other. When this happens, the overall community benefits, the overall community becomes stronger and healthier.

Encouragement

Sometimes it is hard to evangelize new technology.

Well, maybe it isn't hard to evangelize new technology. Maybe it is hard to demonstrate how new technology changes things.

I run into this problem all of the time. I'll meet with a CEO, and the CEO will mention how only 275 individuals are following the company's Twitter presence. The CEO will say that "Twitter doesn't work", mentioning that the company has 175,000 customers who purchased in the past year. The CEO will compare 175,000 customers to 275 followers, concluding that Twitter is just a big waste of time.

I'll also run into a social media expert. This person adores Twitter. She has 48,000 followers, and she generates eighty percent of her consulting revenue from social media. For her, social media works.

Ultimately, the issue of whether social media works or doesn't work has nothing to do with how many followers one has.

The issue, of course, is whether your ecosystem evolves and grows in a direction congruent with business objectives.

This is what most of our real-time measurement systems fail to capture. It's easy to count followers. It's easy to set up a bit.ly link that counts how many individuals click on a link. It's hard to show that demonstrating kindness today results in an improved ecosystem three months from now.

It is my belief that our measurement systems fail to provide us with the information we need to demonstrate that something truly works, or to demonstrate that something truly does not work.

Hashtag Analytics is designed to illustrate that there are different, non-traditional ways to evaluate how a social media ecosystem evolves and changes. Maybe the most important takeaway from Hashtag Analytics is the concept of "ecosystem".

In an ecosystem, changes that happen today yield outcomes that may surprise one a few months from now. Models are created to explain what might happen in the future, and by using the models, individuals are able to mitigate potentially negative outcomes by making subtle changes today.

The same process can be applied to social media ecosystems. Too often, we focus on "influencers" … we try to identify the influencer, then we market to the influencer in an effort to achieve our own objectives. Our analysis suggests that manipulation may or may not work. Our analysis suggests that kindness always works.

What we learned in Hashtag Analytics is that "everybody" is an influencer in some way. This is an enormously liberating finding. The new participant who re-tweets content from an influencer can one day become an influencer if the influencer simply offers kindness in return for the re-tweet! We also learned that influencers don't necessarily maintain influencer status over time, as measured via the "mega participant" metric.

When we view a social media community as an ecosystem, we learn that a community is a living, breathing entity, one that can be shaped, changed, and nurtured by individuals.

Intuitively, this makes logical sense. In fact, it's all too simple, social media experts would tell you that they know this to be the truth.

But show me a methodology that you could take to your CEO to demonstrate this empirically?

Finally, we have a methodology to do this! You are empowered to analyze a community, and you now have the tools necessary to predict what might happen to a community in the future. You have the tools to understand which users can be cultivated in a way that yields a stronger, healthier community.

You have an opportunity to move beyond simple, point-in-time metrics, metrics that may dazzle but ultimately offer no insight into the real dynamics of a social media community. Take advantage of this opportunity! Take this methodology, and run with it … do clever things with the methodology, demonstrate the value of communities in new and innovative ways.

Show the social media community that there is value in what they are doing. Show the critics that vibrant ecosystems yield amazing outcomes!

www.ingramcontent.com/pod-product-compliance
Lightning Source LLC
Chambersburg PA
CBHW060931050326
40689CB00013B/3045